Copyright © 2015 by Doogie Horner
Illustrations copyright © 2015 by Doogie Horner

Library of Congress Cataloging-in-Publication Data is available.

ISBN 978-0-7611-8403-4

Design by Doogie Horner

Workman books are available at special discounts when purchased
in bulk for premiums and sales promotions as well as for fund-
raising or educational use. Special editions or book excerpts can
also be created to specification. For details, contact the Special
Sales Director at the address below, or send an email to
specialmarkets@workman.com.

Workman Publishing Co., Inc.
225 Varick Street
New York, NY 10014-4381
workman.com

WORKMAN is a registered trademark of Workman
Publishing Co., Inc.

Printed in China
First printing September 2015

10 9 8 7 6 5 4 3 2

TABLE OF CATS

Hello, and welcome to *Some Very Interesting Cats Perhaps You Weren't Aware Of*. If you are in fact unacquainted with these fascinating felines, this book will serve as a comprehensive primer.

Surpisingly, I was not considered "interesting" enough to warrant inclusion among these compelling cats, which is why I languish here, in the Preface. Personally, I think I'm fascinating.

In fact, let me show you my moss collection!

STAY THY TONGUE!

MASCOT

Unfortunately, Teddy didn't make the basketball team. "You're too short," the coach said. "And also, you're a cat."

Teddy begged and meowed, until finally the coach said, "Alright, alright! You can't play basketball, but I have another job you can do."

MASTERPIECE

Cat with Bread

Balthasar Veen the Elder

circa 1665

SHMOOPSIE POOPSIE CUTESIE PIE

BIG-BONED

"The vet said Shmoops was dangerously above average. Well, I always knew my Poopsie was special! Jennie got mad because he ate her birthday cake before she got to blow out the candles. 'Well,' I told her, 'what would you have wished for? We already have the cutest little kitty in the whole world!'"

MACKINAW
LUMBERCAT

You could use an ax for logging, sure.
A crosscut saw was faster, if you had
a lumbercat to work each end. And of
course, a chainsaw or feller buncher
could chop down a table leg quicker than
you could hiss—but Mackinaw wasn't
trying to do it quick. He wanted to
feel the grain split beneath his paw.
He used his claws.

BAMBAATAA
BREAK-DANCER

1 BOOGIE LOCK

2 THE TURTLE

3 BACKSPIN

4 HUEVO

SHOW CAT

Commissioner Weir disappeared into the Persian Longhair's fur moments after pinning on the blue ribbon. In the interminable minutes since he said, "Wait, there's something in here," and vanished from sight, no one had been brave enough to go in after him. Regardless, the remaining judges agreed that Nubbins was a stunning example of lilac-point coloration.

IMAGINARY FRIEND

Tommy loved Noodles. They played games and went on hikes through the woods. If it was raining, they'd build sofa cushion forts and pretend they were cowboys defending the Alamo.

"Why can't anyone else see you?" Tommy asked him one day.

"Because," Noodles replied, "nobody else has a dangerous carbon monoxide leak in their bedroom."

OLIVER

NOT A LION

In retrospect, Oliver
regretted growing his
hair long.

PYGMY
LION

BIG GAME HUNTER

Follow me into the Africa room, where
each of my trophies tells a story:
There's the shoelace that almost bit
my ear off. Did you know chipmunks
can spit their venom? They aim for
the eyes. Ha! That loafer's hide was
so thick, my claws couldn't even
pierce it. How many times can one cat
cheat death? Look around you, gentle-
men: The answer is on these walls.

IVORY

ENGLISH MAJOR

Shackled in this gulag, slave to the little black bean, I still strive to create art; I *feel* the Great American Cappuccino waiting to be poured. Yet even here, in this provincial penal colony, the critics hound me. My manager said my nondairy lattes are "too subversive," but it's not my fault—soy milk is inherently satirical! I guess it could be worse, though. I heard Joan Didion used to work at Dunkin' Donuts.

FFFFFSSSSSSHHHHOOOO

SNOWBALL
MOUNTAIN CLIMBER

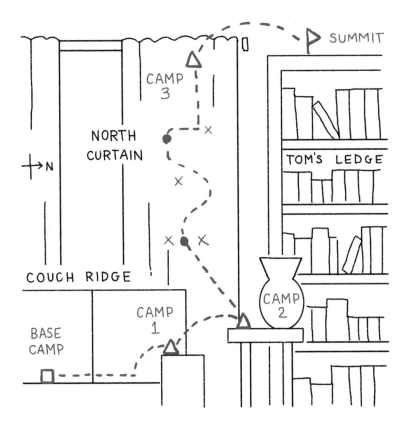

FAMOUS INTERNET KITTEHS

UNO

McCATLEY CULKIN

ME GUSTA

CAPT. CARDBOARD

FRUMPY CAT

CUTESY PEETS

CAT JONG-UN

DOMINO

HEADSTAND HERB

SNAKE
PLISSKEN

THE ORACLE

DOG CAT

GANDALF THE MANX

MR. PEANUT

TROLL CAT

COMBOVER CAT

MYSTERIO

PENNY

WAILING WALLY

AMOEBA

Using a powerful
microscope, we can
see that cats—on the
smallest, most molecular
level—are simply made
up of more cats.

WERECAT

David woke up on the kitchen floor, a paper bag over his head. He'd had that crazy dream again last night. As he poured himself a saucer of milk, he noticed the tatters of his shirt were covered in cat hair. That was odd—he hadn't seen any cats in almost a month, not since that huge, red-eyed tom had bitten him while he was walking on the Scottish moors. David purred quietly as he pondered possible connections.

BOOTS TIDYMAN

DECLAWED

They thought he was
defenseless . . .

They were wrong.

OLIVIA AND OLIVER

FIGURE SKATERS

Olivia and Oliver were moving in perfect harmony. They had just gone through the diagonal step sequence, and were about to enter into the dangerously difficult curve lift, when someone in the sound booth accidentally hit shuffle on their iPod, and the soothing strains of *Swan Lake* were replaced by the distinctive opening guitar riff of "Hot for Teacher."

XORT

ALIEN

Xort's race had conquered countless planets, but none had fallen quite so easily. Already his people had trained the Earthlings to obey their every psychic command.

At night Xort sent updates to the Mothership.

"Have trained my humans to feed and pet me. They suspect nothing."

SOPHISTICATED SINGLE

BREED:
Tabby/Tiger

BODY TYPE:
Furry, soft

DECLAWED?:
Clawed &
LOVING it!!

KITTENS:
12–16, unsure

NEUTERED?:
Tell ya later

LOOKING FOR:
A sunbeam

I'm adventurous! I LOVE water and I can do a perfect cannonball. Caring. Great with kittens. I don't shed at all too much. Gentle. I rarely scratch (unless you want me to!). ;P

OLD FUR AND CLAWS

OLD FUR AND CLAWS
WAR HERO

General Claws was so calm under fire
that he often napped in the saddle, and
won the Battle of Gerbil Hill while
dozing on top of a pleasantly warm
cannon muzzle. His tail had been sheared
off by musket fire, and he kept it tied
around his neck; although it was dismem-
bered, soldiers swore they could still
see it twitch sometimes during battle.

JOEY

(AKA MR. WRINKLES, POOPSY CUTESY POOPS, MISTER PRETTY KITTY, RUFFLES POTATO CHIPS FOREHEAD, WHISKERS MALONE, FUZZY TUMMY, SCRITCH SCRATCH, BIG TUNA, MIKEY GREEN EYES, TOMMY TWO MEOWS, SHEDZ, JOEY CHEEZBURGER, THE COUCH KING, BAD BAD BAD KITTY!, THE BROW, MEOWY PETE, JOEY BAGELS FOR LUNCH, THE COUCH KILLER, MEOWZER, KILLER, SOCKS, SHMOOPY CUTES, SILLY BILLY, THE SILENT MOUSETRAP)

BUSINESSMAN

MINOR DEITY

Other deities always ask me, "You're a Hindu god, right?" Sometimes I'll pretend to get angry and say "NO, I'm GREEK," but honestly, I'm not sure; there are 330 million Hindu gods, so it's hard to keep track. I have four arms like Vishnu (Hindu), but I'm a cat like Bastet (Egyptian), so your guess is as good as mine. Anyhow, if you want to pray to me, go for it. I'll try to help if I can!

BAYOU BOY

UNKLE STINKYS SHACK SMAKIN JAMBALAYA

INGRADIENTS

- mess a' crawdads
- whole heap a' spices
- some beer
- squirrel-sized block a' butter
- frog's blood (fresh)
> Serves 6 cats or just Aunt Sassy

DIRECSHUNS

Mix ever' thing up an hide it in a holler log. Leave 'til it starts tu attract 'gators, then it's dun. Season with donkey sause. Yum!

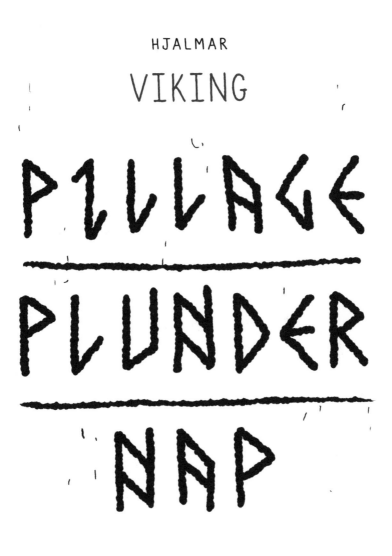

HJALMAR

VIKING

PILLAGE
PLUNDER
NAP

PENNY

PERCEPTIVE

Somewhere in Japan,
Miss Eguchi opened a
can of tuna fish.

MARLEY

GHOST

Marley appeared, translucent and glowing, over Scrooge's bed. He shook his heavy chains. "These are the chains I forged in life!" he howled.

Scrooge batted at the chains with his tiny paw.

"Hey, stop that," Marley said. "Those are metaphors of my greed . . ."

Scrooge rolled over onto his back, still swatting at the spectral chains.

EDISON

MODERN MARVEL

IT WALKS! IT MEOWS!

SEE!   HEAR!

1876

CENTENNIAL
EXHIBITION

PHILA.   PA.

OVER 50
WELSHMEN
DIED DURING ITS
CONSTRUCTION

THE IRON CAT
FIGHT A LIVE
TIGER!

ITS MEOW CURE
A WOMAN OF
CONSUMPTION!

THE
INCREDIBLE

IRON CAT

CHIMAERA

"A creature fearful, of immortal make, is
the chimaera. Flapful wings of terrible
featheriness bedeck her broad back,
and hoofy hooves hoover belowbacks.
Stuck to the hinderparts of this hellish
ungulate is a grim-eyed cat orb, which
breathes forth flameful flames of flame.
Only treats or tummy rubs can stay
the beast's wrath."

—Homer, from *The Iliad*

EIGHTH WONDER
OF THE WORLD

Kong scaled higher and higher, but the puny animals still attacked him.

He thought of his home in the jungle.

He thought of the beautiful little girl who had brought him here to the big city.

Kong bellowed in rage, and then he felt the lamp begin to tip.

HOPELESS ROMANTIC

"What I really want to
do with my life—what I
want to do for a
living—is I want to
be with your daughter.
I'm good at it."

SUPERHERO

Catman has many powers: He can see at night, climb walls, and survive falling from great heights. He has limited immortality (nine lives, although he lost four of them in the X-tinction War Crossover; see *C.R.U.S.H. Puppies* #28). He can cause sneezing and itchy eyes in criminals with allergies and has catlike agility; he also has catlike speed and strength. His nemesis, Dr. Sunbeam, can plunge Catman into a deep sleep.

MARSUPIAL ⌄

CATS OF AUSTRALIA

‹ STUB-LEGGED
WALLA WOO

DANGLY
DOO ›

‹ MUD
BUZZER

KABUKI ACTOR

The rogues surrounded the samurai and beat him with sticks. One grabbed his sword, still in its scabbard, and threw it into the brush.

The samurai thought he was going to die, but then he heard a strong voice yell "Shibaraku!"

The rogues froze. They turned in terror and beheld the fearsome visage of Kagemasa striding toward them.

PHILIPPE, SQUIRT,
XANDO, PIERRE, RENALD,
POUNCE & LANDO

THE
AMAZING
VESPUCCI
BROTHERS

THE CAT OF HEARTS

In 1876 Mad Dog Tannen was shot playing poker in the Pretty Pony while holding a stack of flapjacks, two mop squeezers, and the Calico King (as the Cat of Hearts is commonly called), and ever since then the Man with the Yarn has been considered bad luck. Whether you call him Ted Nugent, Little Slick, or the Devil's Toothbrush, most players just call him "The Door," cuz he's the last thing you see before you hit the street.

MR. STITCHES
CREEPY PUPPET

"You're a real dummy, you know that?"

"Yes, Mr. Stitches."

"I gotta think for both of us, don't I?"

"I guess so."

"If only I could break the curse that keeps me in this wooden prison, I would rule as I did in the Old Days!"

"Yes, Mr. Stitches."

"Oh, well . . . We're on in three. Straighten my bowtie."

PRISONER

He didn't have a name. He was Kitten Number 6. At night he sawed the bars with a nail file, but his progress was slow. Five kittens were born before him. Five brothers and sisters. And every day he watched as they were carried away by smiling children—borne to what terrible fate he did not know. He didn't have a name, but he did have a dream: freedom.

SEA CAPTAIN

The captain had weathered countless storms. Each time, he had crawled from the tub sodden, shaking—but alive. He could always tell when a squall was brewing . . .

And he sensed one now.

MR. BIGGLE

YOUR BOSS

Ron was in big trouble. He had bungled the Browne deal, and now he was going to get yelled at by Mr. Biggle himself. Although Ron saw Biggle's name on the building when he walked into work each morning, he'd never seen his boss in person. Entering his office now, he finally understood why everyone whispered "Watch out: Biggle's one tough kitten."

ROCK STAR

GUITAR WEEKLY: Most rock stars have a ton of groupies—but not you. Are the rumors true? Are you neutered?

ZIGGY: Oh no, I'm still swinging a hammer. But I'll tell you what else I'm doing, Steve: I'm playing my guitar. Every night I make love to her on stage. If she saw me with another woman, well, I don't know—she might get jealous.

RONALD

CATFISH

Most cats
didn't like water.

But Ronald wasn't
like most cats.

CONSTELLATION

Cattus Major is visible year-round in the Northern Hemisphere. It is the rarely used thirteenth sign of the zodiac, reserved for people born on February 29 during leap years. In medieval times, people born under this sign were considered "consorts of the devil." Famous Cattuses include Liza Minnelli and Art Garfunkel.

DINOSAUR

Millions of years ago, giants roamed the Earth. Of all these fuzzy wuzzy titans, the most deadly and adorable was *Tabbysaurus rex*: the Thunder Kitty. Its razor-sharp claws were over three feet long, and scientists have concluded—after careful study of the fossil record—that its fur was probably super soft and pettable.

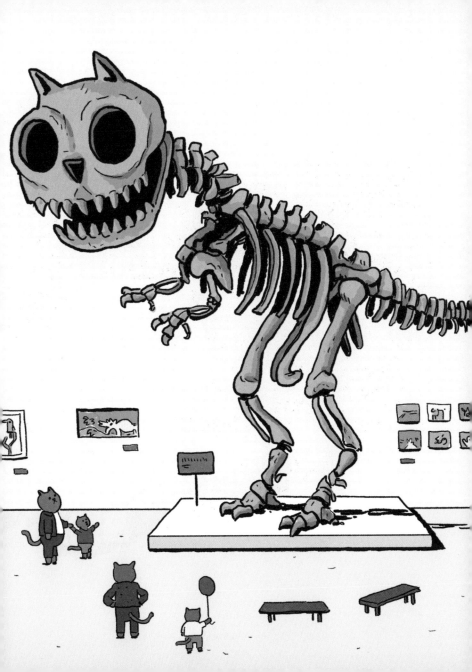

SHADOWCAT

Stephen knew that people called him a scaredy-cat. They said that he was afraid of his own shadow.

Well, they were right.

MR. TIBBLES

MASTER OF DISGUISE

At the gilded doors outside the opera house, Mr. Tibbles was stopped by security. "No cats allowed!" the guard barked.

From inside, Mr. Tibbles could hear the overture of *The Magic Flute* just beginning.

He was in a panic until the Duchess of Worcestershire patted him on the head and whispered, "Don't worry, I know how to sneak you inside."

THAG

CAVECAT

Cave drawing of mouse hunt,

circa 5000 B.C.

SASSY, JOEY, REX, AND WIGGLES

HOMEWARD BOUND

They paused to catch their breath at the top of the hill. Sassy surveyed the landscape, miles of forests and mountains stretching to the horizon. He knew they'd find their master no matter how far they had to travel. Joey whistled a chipper song and Rex barked, everyone eager to get moving again. They were so happy and confident, it was hard to believe that by nightfall they'd all be dead.

JAPANESE LUCKY CAT

A samurai was walking to the Gotokuji
Temple when a smiling cat beckoned to
him from a shop window. The samurai
entered the shop and bought a bottle
of sword polish and a lottery ticket
that ended up winning 1.5 pounds of
gold powder (current value $35,000).
Ever since then, cats have been
considered wise and lucky spirits.

HIDEOUS STRAY

"Oh look, honey, there's a cat on the porch."

"Lemme see—oh god! What *is* it?!"

"The poor kitty looks hungry."

"I can smell it through the door!"

"I'll get a saucer of milk."

"Its eye! Like the lidless orb of Sauron, burning into my brain!"

"Here we go, I've got a nice bowl of milk."

"It doesn't want milk, Marcia. It wants our souls!!"

CARRIE, BROOKE & JESSICA

MEAN GIRLS

YOU CAN'T SIT WITH US!

RIPLEY

EVIL TWIN

"Dickie's been acting weird lately."

"What do you mean?"

"Well, last night I woke up and saw him standing at the foot of our bed."

"What was he doing?"

"Nothing, nothing. He was just standing there and . . . watching us. Watching us sleep."

"Huh. Weird."

MURF!

JASPER

MUMMY

"Sarah! The darn cat is playing with the toilet paper again!"

"Is he doing the mummy thing? Take a video!"

"I don't think we should encourage him . . ."

"But Tim, he's got talent!"

"For the last time: I'm not paying for acting lessons. *He's going to law school.*"

YOSHI

NINJA

SILENT AS A SHADOW

WEIGHTLESS AS

MOONLIGHT.

STRIKE

WITHOUT WARNING

DEADLY

AS A MOUSETRAP.

RUSSIAN NESTING CAT

Evening prayers drifted down from the minarets. Igor belted a shot of vodka and twisted the head off the doll, revealing a smaller one inside.

"Within each cat, another cat," he said. "New truths are revealed. Others remain hidden."

James was tired of riddles. "Speaking of truth," he pressed, "tell me: Where's the microfilm?"

Suddenly, a shot rang out!

MAGICIAN

The Magnificent Mystico had lots of famous illusions—The Yarn of Doom, Multiplying Mice, King Tut's Tomb—but nobody could figure out how he did his big finale, the one where he sawed a dog in half. The answer was simple: He didn't like dogs.

PRAIRIE CATS

MITTS

POLITICIAN

Being a Democat came naturally to Mitts. He had no problem toeing the party line. He was pro-sunbeam, pro-tuna, and anti-bath. He believed in lower countertops and higher scratching posts, and supported increased funding for both yarn and laser-pointer research.

There was only one part of his job he couldn't stand: the darn kittens.

FENG SHUI GRIP

KITTYTRON

AGES 5+
FULLY POSABLE

TRANSFORMER

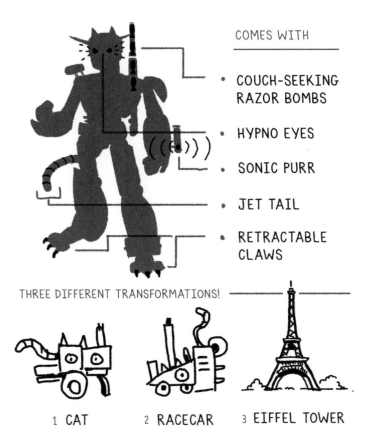

COMES WITH

- COUCH-SEEKING RAZOR BOMBS

- HYPNO EYES

- SONIC PURR

- JET TAIL

- RETRACTABLE CLAWS

THREE DIFFERENT TRANSFORMATIONS!

1 CAT   2 RACECAR   3 EIFFEL TOWER

121

TOM

ACTOR

Tom loved acting, and he loved cats. But he discovered something about himself after performing on Broadway for ten years: He did not love acting like a cat.

TROJAN CAT

"This is awesome! Let's wheel it inside."

"I don't know, I've got a bad feeling about this. Look at my nose! It's twitching like crazy."

"C'mon, don't be such a scaredy-cat."

"PLEASE don't say that word."

PRINCESS

Fluffkins was the prettiest cat in the kingdom, but none of the princes would marry her because they were all human. So the king threw a gala that included an open bar. "She's actually quite pretty —for a cat," Prince Pembroke said after five Appletinis. "Her nose is so shapely," Prince Brandon mumbled beside him. It was the last thing he remembered until the next morning, when he woke to find Fluffkins curled at the foot of his bed.

R'LYEH

GILMAN

CTHULHU

PH'NGLUI
MGLW'NAFH

CTHULHU
R'LYEH WGAH'

NAGL
FHTAGN

RIGGS

UNDERCOVER COP

Riggs had been embedded with the pack for a long time—maybe too long. He was starting to enjoy the taste of Milk-Bones, and that scared him. His captain was worried, too. During their last meeting, he'd caught Riggs wagging his tail.

"That's alright, Riggs," the captain had said. "Just make sure the tail isn't wagging you."

BUZZ

ASTRONAUT

CAMERON

DREAMBOAT

BREED: Mom was a blue-ribbon Scottish Fold; Dad was a tomcat.

FAVE THING TO SCRATCH: Records! Ha, ha.

MY PERFECT CAT: Don't care what she looks like, as long as she's gorgeous.

BIGGEST FEAR: Vacuum cleaners.

PETS: Three little girls (the outdoor kind).

BEST QUALITY: My cute little pink nose.

SUPERPOWER I'D LOVE TO HAVE: The ability to reach out and pet every kitty who listens to my records.

VERY FLUFFY

A crisp fall breeze ruffled Fluffy's fur.
It felt good. She closed her eyes as the
wind picked up. She felt so light. She
wondered why her owners had never let
her outside before, and then she opened
her eyes.

LOKI

KLEPTOMANIAC

They both froze: Kevin with his hand on the doorknob, Loki with Kevin's tooth-brush in his mouth. The bathroom was silent except for the dripping faucet. The clock radio clicked on in the bedroom; the warm harmonies of Martha and the Vandellas echoed down the hall, and Loki knew there was nowhere to run to, baby, nowhere to hide.

PHIL

HIGHER POWER

In the beginning, Phil created a ball of
yarn. And Phil batted the yarn around
for a little while, and he saw that it was
good. And then he was like, "Well, this
is fun, but if I don't get started on the
rest of the universe this could take
all week."

RECLUSIVE AUTHOR

Even in his own home, the mysterious author of *The Dogcatcher's Daughter* is rarely seen.

"He's usually hiding under the sofa," his owner, Miss M., says. "Sometimes I can't find him for days, and then I'll open the dryer and he'll hop out. He's a very shy kitty!"

Regarding her cat's literary output, Miss M. is rather evasive herself, saying only, "I don't read cat books."

DON'T CALL ME MEGAN

REBELLIOUS TEEN

I wish my mother had

drowned me

in a bucket.

Litter is just a synonym

for *refuse*.

Nine lives equal nine deaths.

"Spay me, Dark Lord," I yowl

at the moon . . . alone.

LARS

WEIGHT LIFTER

The world's strongest cat is Lars
Leetaru of Junction, Utah. He can
deadlift a ball of thick-gauge yarn
(3 kg.), flip a full box of cookies off
a kitchen counter (125 oz.), and pull a
wagon with a small, terrified dog in
it the length of a living room. His mass-
building diet includes drinking lots of
milk right before taking a long nap.

HOUSE CAT

Eve came by to "borrow" some milk yesterday, and she asked me, "Isn't it boring to be a house cat?" I suppose she thinks living outside, eating field mice, and sleeping in trash cans makes her some kind of worldly sage. Well, I've seen what's outside. I have a big bay window whose glass I keep very clean. Sometimes birds fly into it and break their poor little necks.

RRRRR

FORMER CHILD STAR

FILMOGRAPHY

1988: *Little Stinkers; Shipoppi; The Tiniest President; The Fun Squad!*

1989: *Mummy Dad; Bummer School*

1992: *Teens in Space* (voice of Principal Zurg); *Butt Police 3, Dog Lovers*

1996: *Candy Snatchers* (uncredited)

2000: *Smut Bordello; Bikini Zombies*

2008: *Corey Quinn: Uncensored* (documentary); *Sunset Strippers*

2014: *Little Stinkers 2* (Off-Broadway)

CAESAR

EMPEROR

"CRY HAVOC, AND LET SLIP THE CATS OF WAR"

154

PSYCHO

Boots hid in the shadows, tracking his prey. He was a lion. He was a panther. He was vengeance wrought in feline form. He was claw and tooth, bright and quick, aflame with feeling. No eye could frame his fearful symmetry. He hid in the shadows. Then his prey wandered past and he could smell the blood just below its skin—and he pounced.

ROGER

CONSULTANT

What do I consult on? Well, as an accredited associate, I confabulate in a wide variety of sectors, but I specialize in performance consultation vis-à-vis conduit optimization. My expert advice primarily consists of initiative execution—not to be misconstrued as sector analysis/input.

Confusing you say? Perhaps . . . perhaps to the *uneducated*. Of course, that's why people hire me.

CAT?

The animal arrived at Petco in an unmarked carrier, and the staff was immediately faced with a dilemma: They didn't know what section of the store to place it in. Was it a bat? Or maybe a . . . vole? Tom suggested using the process of elimination, so after carefully checking the thing for feathers, they confidently crossed "bird" off their list, then ran to fill up a fish tank.

RANDY

ELASTICAT

LOGAN
COSPLAYER

earholes

SKI MASK

x2   x2   x4

CARDBOARD

TAPE

PAPER
x 2

MOON BOOTS

PAINT (blue)

MITTENS

cut holes
x6

silverware

CATNIP ENTHUSIAST

We were somewhere
around Barstow on the
edge of the desert
when the 'nip began
to take hold.

TATTOO

"Bro, what's that, is that a tattoo?"

"Oh, uh, no."

"Dude, it looked like a tattoo."

"It was, but it's nothing."

"What's it a tattoo of?"

"It's a . . . tiger. Fighting a python."

"Really? Because it looked like it was

a . . . sexy cat lady or something."

"Ha! That's crazy. No, no, no. Tiger and

snake. Hey, you need another beer, bro?"

PEPPER

CURIOUS

1. How does a lawn mower work?

2. Is that bulldog friendly?

3. How high can I climb in this tree?

4. What's the inside of the clothes dryer smell like?

5. What does antifreeze taste like?

6. Why do my owners tell me not to nap under the car?

7. Can I fly?

8. How many rubber bands can I eat?

9. Do I really have nine lives?

MUFFIN

ALARM CLOCK

FEED.

ME.

NOW.

TREASURE MAP

The isle is named for the deadly reefs, sharp as claws, which surround it, so you must enter at Whisker's Inlet. Hook east 'round the shoulder of Fuzz Mountain, down into Tummy Wummy Valley and past the Shedding Forest until you reach the Southern Haunch.

The treasure lies at the southern end of the island, inside a rank cavern the natives, for whatever reason, call Cat Butt Cove.

CLAW ISLAND

BAY OF PAWS

LUCKY WHISKERS

ACTION HERO

IN

NINE LIVES

VIII

EIGHT DOWN...
ONE TO GO.

CURIOSITY PICTURES AND PURRFECT ENTERTAINMENT INC. LLC.
PRESENT A MR. SOX PICTURE DIRECTED BY MR. SOX MUSIC BY TIBBLES
EDITOR CUTESIE POOTSIE, A.C.E. PRODUCTION DESIGNER SNOWBALL

SCOOTER
DAREDEVIL

The trick was less dangerous than it looked. Toby was a well-trained dog, and Scooter had a metal plate in his head ever since his famous Clothes Dryer of Doom stunt went wrong. But Toby was still an animal, and Scooter knew someday Toby would give in to his instincts and eat him. That was alright though. The ride was wild while it lasted.

COCO

FASHION VICTIM

"Let the kid give Coco
a haircut," they said.
"What's the worst
that could happen?"
they said.

SPIRIT ANIMAL

The seeker had fasted for three hours, and was getting light-headed. He crawled into his sacred sweat lodge—a Toyota sitting in the sun with all the windows rolled up—and ate the shiitake mushrooms he'd found growing fuzz under the fridge.

His mind opened like a lotus. He saw fire in an ancient forest, and his spirit animal rose up before him through the smoke. Secretly, he was disappointed it wasn't a bear.

COOL DAD

"Hey son, what's up? Can we hang for a sec? Look, I know it's gnarly being a teenager. Your body is changing, you're starting to think about girls—or boys, whatever—you're experimenting with e-cigarettes—I've been there. I've listened to Pink Floyd. I just want you to know that if you need someone to rap with, I'm cool. Oh, and yo: Can you accept my friend request? Otherwise I can't see your wall."

MIXED BREED

Suddenly the creature was illuminated by a flash of lightning.

"My god, doctor," his assistant gasped, "What is it!?"

"It's a Himalayan Longhair/Egyptian Shorthair/Scottish Fold/Maine Coon/ Siamese/Persian mix."

"Its pedigree is an abomination!"

"Pedigree?" He laughed, thunder booming outside. "What pedigree?"

PANT
PANT

STAR-CROSSED LOVERS

My bounty is as
boundless as
the sea,
My love as deep;
the more I give to thee,
The more I have,
for both are infinite.

YOUR TRUE SELF

Todd removed all the mirrors from his home, but he couldn't stay inside forever, so occasionally he'd round a corner somewhere and come face-to-face with a grizzled stranger—realizing only after a confused moment that the stranger was himself.

That was okay, though. More troubling were the times when he recognized the stranger immediately—and far too well.

WILD AT HEART

Morowa heard something. She lifted her bloody maw from the kill and scanned the savannah: senegals and jackleberries dotting brown hills that rolled to a shimmering horizon. She was just about to resume feeding when she heard it again. It was a strange noise, one that didn't belong here. It almost sounded like . . . a can opener.

WIRRRRRR

HELMUT

ARTIST

My work grapples with the loss of identity quadrupeds suffer under the oppressive pedagogy of a bipedal society. A dead bird in a shoe; a baby's breath stolen at night; a hair sculpture made by my stomach: These totems deconstruct cultural norms like witches' consorts and YouTube jesters and recapture our bestial essence.

ROMERO

PERSISTENT

The cat came back
the very next day.

The cat came back,
we thought he was a goner.

But the cat came back.

He just wouldn't stay away.

AGORAPHOBIC

"Tucker *loves* going for walks."

"Really? It doesn't look like he enjoys it."

"Sure he does! Look, he's shaking with joy!"

"He's really digging those claws into the ground, huh?"

"Well, he's excited. He knows we're going to the pool."

SUPERVILLAIN

He had a secret lair inside a volcano, the magma cleverly diverted so it flowed down the walls. He had a black yacht with a mini-sub and helicopter. He had a thousand henchmen, each of them a master of kung fu. He even had a cool scar! In a sudden moment of clarity he realized that he had . . . everything. Everything he had ever wanted.

He pressed the intercom button. "Cancel the evil scheme. I'm content."

BIG FAN

Claw, Bobcats, claw

Claw your way to the top!

Scratch, Bobcats, scratch

Scratch and screech and never stop!

We will nap briefly at halftime,

and nap after the game,

but we'll never, never, never nap

(trumpet solo)

UNTIL VICTORY WE CLAIM!

JUST A NORMAL CAT

I am a totally normal cat! I am not superintelligent or the next phase in evolution. I am not the cat you saw on the news, the one who escaped from a government lab. You can get me wet and feed me after midnight, because I am just a normal cat you should leave unattended near a computer, your car keys, and 2 kg. of refined plutonium.

Meow! I'm a cat.

DOOGIE HORNER'S previous books include *Everything Explained Through Flowcharts* and *100 Ghosts*. You can find him online at doogiehorner.com.

THE AUTHOR WOULD LIKE TO THANK Jennie Thwing, Jason Rekulak, and Peter Steinberg. Also of course Bruce Tracy, Janet Vicario, Ariana Abud, Marta Jaremko, and all the other wonderful people at Workman Publishing.